MW01138057

AMERICAN DEMOCRACY
in Crisis

Naomi Rockler

ReferencePoint
Press

San Diego, CA

© 2024 ReferencePoint Press, Inc.
Printed in the United States

For more information, contact:
ReferencePoint Press, Inc.
PO Box 27779
San Diego, CA 92198
www.ReferencePointPress.com

LIBRARY OF CONGRESS CATALOGING-IN-PUBLICATION DATA

Names: Rockler, Naomi, author.
Title: American democracy in crisis / by Naomi Rockler.
Description: San Diego, CA : ReferencePoint Press, Inc., 2024. | Includes
    bibliographical references and index.
Identifiers: LCCN 2023028339 (print) | LCCN 2023028340 (ebook) | ISBN
    9781678207229 (library binding) | ISBN 9781678207236 (ebook)
Subjects: LCSH: Democracy--United States--History--Juvenile literature. |
    Communication in politics--Juvenile literature. | Elections--United
    States--History--Juvenile literature. | Political participation--Social
    aspects--United States--Juvenile literature.
Classification: LCC JK1726 .R64 2024 (print) | LCC JK1726 (ebook) | DDC
    320.47309--dc23/eng/20230727
LC record available at https://lccn.loc.gov/2023028339
LC ebook record available at https://lccn.loc.gov/2023028340

CONTENTS

A Crisis Point for American Democracy

Many Americans take the peaceful transition of power from one president to the next for granted. The process seems straightforward; the people elect a president, and on Inauguration Day, the new president moves into the White House and the previous one leaves.

However, on January 6, 2021, Americans saw firsthand that the peaceful transition of power is nothing to take for granted. Protesters broke into the US Capitol Building for the purpose of overturning the results of the 2020 presidential election. Incumbent president Donald Trump had been defeated by former vice president Joe Biden. Trump claimed—without evidence—that the election was stolen due to voter fraud. He repeated that unsubstantiated claim many times.

January 6 was the day that the election results were scheduled to be certified by Congress—normally a routine procedural step. On that day protesters who believed Trump's claims of a stolen election marched to the Capitol. The protest turned into an insurrection—a term that refers to a violent uprising against a government—when over two thousand protesters forced their way into the building. Fearing for their safety, members of Congress halted the election certification proceedings and sheltered in place per the instructions of the US Capitol Police. Many congressional representatives were terrified, like California representative Sara Jacobs, who said, "We could hear the mob behind us and Capitol police running, and that's when I was really scared. I really thought that we were going to be killed."[1]

The scene was brutal. Capitol police were outnumbered but fought back. "I saw friends with blood all over their faces," Officer Caroline Edwards told members of the House of Representatives' January 6 Committee. "I was slipping in people's blood."[2] Some insurrectionists smeared feces on the walls. Others called for Vice President Mike Pence to be hanged—and fashioned a noose—because Pence refused to invalidate the election. One of the most shocking images was an insurrectionist in the Capitol carrying a Confederate flag—a symbol of rebellion against the United States. Four people died that day and the next—three insurrectionists and one police officer—and 138 officers were injured.

> "We could hear the mob behind us and Capitol police running, and that's when I was really scared. I really thought that we were going to be killed."[1]
>
> —Sara Jacobs, California representative

The insurrection ended around seven o'clock that evening, and Congress reconvened later that evening to certify the election. However, that was not the end of the crisis. Since January 6, serious challenges to democracy have continued, including violent threats against election officials and efforts to suppress voting.

Basic Principles

A democratic nation is one in which ordinary people determine how they wish to be governed. Unlike a dictatorship or other authoritarian regime, which function according to the wishes of the person who holds power, citizens in a democracy make governing choices through their elected representatives. America has never been a perfect democracy in which everyone has a voice. For example, women could not vote until 1920, and Black people were enslaved until the Civil War and restricted from voting in many states until the 1960s. In fact, America is technically a *democratic republic*, which means that decisions are made directly by politicians—but those politicians are given power by the people who elect them.

However, perfect or not, a fundamental part of being American has always been respect for the basic principles of democracy. These principles include the freedom to vote and express political opinions. They also include the belief that everyone should be treated equally under the law and that people with unpopular opinions have the same rights as people with popular ones.

Democracy is never guaranteed. As political scientist Erica Chenoweth argues, "In order to have democracy, all major political players in that democracy—in this case, all political parties—have to agree on some fundamental norms. The first is that they accept the results of elections. The second is that they reject the use of violence as a legitimate part of the political process, especially in establishing who is going to govern."[3]

Both of these norms were challenged on January 6, when election results were rejected violently. These norms continue to erode.

On January 6, 2021, rioters stormed the US Capitol in an attempt to overturn the results of the 2020 presidential election. January 6 marked a crisis point for American democracy.

In a 2022 NBC News poll, about one-third of all Americans—and two-thirds of Republicans—said that the 2020 presidential election results were not legitimate. Moreover, in a 2022 National Public Radio poll, about a quarter of Americans said that political violence is sometimes justified.

Another fundamental norm that democracy depends on is the willingness of people to work together for the good of society. While political disagreements are a sign of a healthy democracy, the demonization of political opponents is a sign of a democracy in trouble. Today many Democrats and Republicans are willing to fight for their party's positions at all costs—even if that means going against democratic norms.

An Uncertain Future

January 6 was a crisis point for American democracy. However, the crisis did not end that day. This is an unusual and frightening time in American history. Many of the democratic norms of American society—like trust in the legitimacy of elections, and the willingness of legislators from different parties to work together—have shifted. American democracy is at a turning point, and the future is uncertain.

CHAPTER ONE

A Polarized Nation

Jerry misses his siblings. They unfriended him on Facebook and changed their phone numbers because of Jerry's political views. "It wasn't always like this," says Jerry. "We were once a tight knit group."[4]

Jeff Jackson, a North Carolinian elected to Congress in November 2022, describes his workplace as a hostile environment. Many Democrats and Republicans hate each other so much that they refuse to even make small talk. Jackson, a Democrat, had a conversation with a Republican colleague about working together—and kept this conversation secret because he did not want to embarrass the Republican.

There have always been Americans who have political debates at the Thanksgiving table, and there have always been members of Congress who clash with each other on policies and actions. However, in recent years, something has shifted. Civil debates about issues have gotten personal. For many Americans, people with different opinions are the enemy. This level of polarization is a threat to democracy. When people see each other as the enemy—on an interpersonal or government level—it is very difficult to work together on behalf of society as a whole.

What Defines the Right and the Left?

One sign that Americans have become more polarized is that, according to a 2022 Gallup opinion poll, fewer Americans define themselves as centrist or moderate. More Americans define themselves as either right wing or left wing. While not everyone in these categories has the same views, historically there are some typical viewpoints associated with the right and the left.

People on the right (usually Republicans) value individual responsibility, as opposed to reliance on the government. They support lower taxes, limited regulation on businesses, and limited government spending on programs like education and housing. They typically oppose abortion, gun control, same-sex marriage, and an expansion of immigration. They value law and order.

People on the left (usually Democrats) believe the government should help create a more equitable society. They support higher taxes on corporations and wealthy individuals and more government spending on programs like education, health care, housing, and the environment. They typically support abortion rights, gun control, and government-funded health care.

Animosity Between the Right and the Left

In recent years personal animosity between people from the right and left has grown. According to a 2022 Pew Research Center study, "Partisan polarization has long been a fact of political life in the United States. But increasingly, Republicans and Democrats view not just the opposing party but also the *people* in that party in a negative light."[5] In this study, the majority of Democrats and Republicans described people from the other party as dishonest, immoral, closed-minded, and unintelligent.

Much of the angriest debate centers on conflicting values and visions of American life, which is sometimes called the culture war. People on the right often feel nostalgic for a time when America was more traditional and seemed like a simpler culture—a sentiment encapsulated by Donald Trump's "Make America Great Again" slogan. People on the left value cultural change, especially when it comes to equity and inclusion for people of color, women, LGBTQ people, and other minorities.

> "Partisan polarization has long been a fact of political life in the United States. But increasingly, Republicans and Democrats view not just the opposing party but also the *people* in that party in a negative light."[5]
>
> —Pew Research Center

Partisan Hostility Adds to an Already Divided Nation

The divide between Democrats and Republicans goes beyond different social and political views. According to a 2022 Pew Research Center poll, people do not just disagree with the other party's politics, they hold negative views of each other. The poll found that a large number of Republicans view Democrats as immoral, dishonest, and lazy while a large number of Democrats view Republicans as closeminded, dishonest, and immoral.

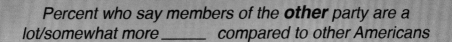

*Percent who say members of the **other** party are a lot/somewhat more _____ compared to other Americans*

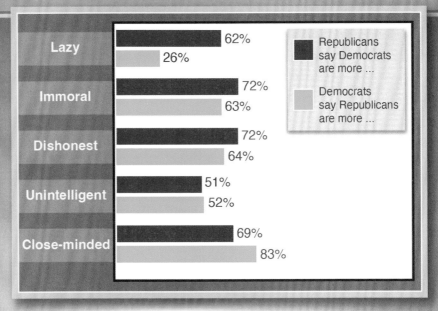

	Republicans say Democrats are more ...	Democrats say Republicans are more ...
Lazy	62%	26%
Immoral	72%	63%
Dishonest	72%	64%
Unintelligent	51%	52%
Close-minded	69%	83%

Source: "As Partisan Hostility Grows, Signs of Frustration with the Two-Party System," Pew Research Center, August 9, 2022. www.pewresearch.org.

These divergent views have led to heated debates about issues like whether transgender people should be allowed to use the bathroom of their choice, whether libraries should offer books about LGBTQ themes for teenagers, and how schools should teach students about racism. Democrats accuse Republicans of being racist, homophobic, transphobic, and hateful. Republicans accuse Democrats of pushing "woke" values on others, and of being "snowflakes" who are oversensitive and offended by everything.

Different Realities

Disagreement about issues is a sign of a healthy democracy. For example, if people in a community disagree on whether there should be a local tax increase, the ongoing debate might help people make more informed decisions when they vote.

Unfortunately, America has become so polarized that many Americans do not just disagree about issues or about how to interpret information that is widely regarded as factual. Instead, they disagree about what information should be regarded as factual and what information should be considered false. It is difficult to have meaningful debate between people who have different views of reality.

One of these issues is the COVID-19 crisis. Throughout the pandemic, Americans had polarized opinions about whether social distancing and masks were effective ways to stop the spread. The degree to which these measures worked is not an opinion; this is something that can be measured scientifically. Nonetheless, Americans disagree on the facts. According to a 2022 Pew Research Center study, Americans were split down the middle about whether social distancing and masks were effective, with Republicans much more likely to say these measures were not effective. Throughout the pandemic, disagreements about how to respond to COVID led to angry debates at gatherings such as city council meetings about whether communities and schools should require masks.

This is also the case with the ongoing issue of COVID-19 vaccinations. According to the Centers for Disease Control and Prevention and the US Food and Drug Administration, COVID vaccines are safe and effective at preventing serious or fatal cases of COVID. Even so, not everyone agrees. Democrats are much more likely to say that vaccines are effective and safe than are Republicans. According to a Morning Consult poll from March 2023, 32 percent of Republicans have chosen not to get vaccinated—as opposed to 9 percent of Democrats. The states where Americans

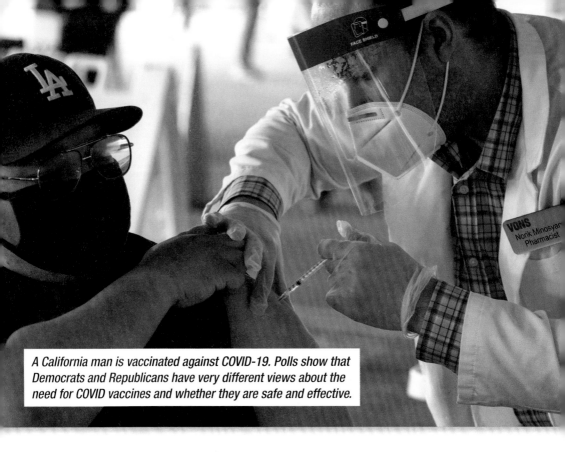

A California man is vaccinated against COVID-19. Polls show that Democrats and Republicans have very different views about the need for COVID vaccines and whether they are safe and effective.

are least likely to get vaccines are majority Republican states, like Idaho and Montana.

Americans also have strongly divergent views regarding the results of the 2020 presidential election. According to a March 2023 CNN poll, 63 percent of Republicans do not believe that Biden was the legitimate winner. On social media, countless people continue to debate the facts of the 2020 election. One conservative Twitter user tweeted in May 2023, "Fact is, there's way more evidence that points to the fact that Trump won the election, than what leftist democrats can cite for Biden, the anomalies are too many to list."[6] In contrast, a liberal user tweeted, "Facts are the facts! Biden won fair and square! You've been trying to prove the election was stolen for 2 years already and you came up with nothing."[7]

Why are Americans so polarized about facts? In a polarized America, many people live in political silos. That is, they are surrounded almost exclusively by others with similar worldviews. "We share space with people with whom we agree on issues political, ideological, religious and cultural," explains journalist Richard Groves. "Behind the hardened walls of our silos, we don't read books, subscribe to newspapers, listen to podcasts or have meaningful conversations with people we don't agree with."[8] If a person grows up in a community where everyone has the same views and is told that the other side is the enemy, it can be difficult to even consider a different perspective.

> "Behind the hardened walls of our silos, we don't read books, subscribe to newspapers, listen to podcasts or have meaningful conversations with people we don't agree with."[8]
>
> —Richard Groves, journalist

Political Paralysis

Sarah Huckabee Sanders, the Republican governor of Arkansas, embodied the level of hostility between the right and the left when she said, "The dividing line in America is no longer between right and left—it's between normal and crazy."[9] In fact, it is easy to imagine a Democrat making the same polarizing statement, only with the intent of ascribing craziness to the right.

When each side sees itself as normal and the other side as crazy—as opposed to seeing each other as well-intentioned and

A Politician Denounced by His Family

A chilling example of what happens when someone in politics breaks with an official party position is Adam Kinzinger, a former Republican member of Congress from Illinois. After January 6, Kinzinger became a vocal opponent of Donald Trump. He was one of only ten congressional Republicans who voted to impeach Trump for his role in the January 6 insurrection. He was shunned by the Republicans and did not run for reelection. Most striking, though, was the way that Kinzinger was shunned by his own family members for speaking out against Trump. The New York Times printed a handwritten letter to Kinzinger from eleven of his family members, repeatedly calling him a bad Christian and accusing him of joining "the devil's army." The letter said, in part, "Oh my, what a disappointment you are to us and to God! . . . It is now most embarrassing to us that we are related to you. You have embarrassed the Kinzinger family name!"

Quoted in New York Times, "Read the Letter from Several of Kinzinger's Family Members," February 15, 2021. www.nytimes.org.

rational—then working together to solve problems is a challenge that is sometimes insurmountable. The us-versus-them hostility between Democrats and Republicans has led to what sociologist Michael Macy calls political paralysis. "The most likely outcome of increasing polarization is political paralysis in which the parties are more interested in winning than in solving problems," argues Macy. "We have heard politicians even feel so emboldened that they can publicly acknowledge that their goal is obstruction, not problem solving."[10]

> "The most likely outcome of increasing polarization is political paralysis in which the parties are more interested in winning than in solving problems."[10]
>
> —Michael Macy, sociologist

For example, Republican senator Mitch McConnell, the Senate minority leader, has been vocal about his goal to obstruct the Biden administration. "One-hundred percent of my focus is on standing up to this administration," said McConnell shortly after Biden took office. "What we have in the United States Senate is [total] unity from Susan Collins to Ted Cruz in opposition to what the new Biden administration is trying to do to this country."[11]

McConnell is not alone. In Congress, Republicans and Democrats alike feel increased pressure to fully support their party's official positions. In the past, it was more common for legislators to vote for positions that were unpopular with their party. In 2009, for example, a sizable number of congressional Democrats opposed many of the party's positions on abortion. That year sixty-four Democrats voted for an amendment to the Affordable Care Act to guarantee that abortions would not be federally funded. However, as of 2023 Henry Cuellar of Texas was the only antiabortion Democrat in Congress.

Today, when members of Congress defy party lines, they face serious consequences. An example of this is former Wyoming representative Liz Cheney, a prominent Republican who voted to impeach Trump for his role in the January 6 insurrection and served as vice chair of the House committee to investigate Trump's role in that event. Cheney was shunned by her party.

House Select Committee Vice Chair Liz Cheney, a Wyoming Republican, speaks during the committee's investigation into the January 6, 2021, attack on the Capitol. Cheney was shunned by her party and lost reelection because of her role in the investigation.

In the following election, she lost the Wyoming Republican primary election and was replaced in Congress by a strong Trump supporter. This kind of pressure—to adhere to party lines or risk losing one's job—makes it even harder for the two parties to work together.

Why Political Paralysis Is a Threat to Democracy

Political paralysis is harmful to democracy for several reasons. When legislators refuse to compromise, it is very hard to pass legislation and budgets or complete other work on behalf of the people. Macy argues that this was especially a problem during the COVID-19 pandemic, in Congress and also in local government. Because Democrats and Republicans were at odds with each other about things like mask mandates, they were unable to work together to minimize the impact of the crisis.

Another problem with political paralysis in Congress is that it encourages presidents to rely on executive orders to get things done. Executive orders are presidential directives used to manage US government operations. Although they have the force of law, they do not require congressional debate or approval. Every president has issued at least one executive order. Recent presidents have issued executive orders for actions that might not have won congressional approval. For example, Trump signed an executive order to build a wall on the US-Mexico border, and Biden signed an executive order to stop building it. Congress—which is supposed to be part of the constitutional system of checks and balances that keeps the president from becoming too powerful—did not have a say in either decision.

Political paralysis also impacts the Supreme Court. Supreme Court justices, who serve for life, are nominated by the president. The Senate interviews the nominee and then votes on whether he or she should become a member of the court. In the past many

Civility Breaks Down in Presidential Addresses to Congress

The norm for presidential speeches to Congress used to be civility. Members showed their disagreement by not applauding for something the president said, but that was it. This changed in 2009 during a speech to Congress by President Barack Obama. When Obama made a comment about immigration, Representative Joe Wilson from South Carolina loudly yelled, "You lie!" This lack of civility was also present in 2020 at President Donald Trump's State of the Union address. At the end of the speech, Speaker of the House Nancy Pelosi ripped her copy of the speech into pieces, saying later that it was full of lies. This incivility continued during the 2023 State of the Union address, at which dozens of Republicans repeatedly booed and heckled President Joe Biden. For example, Tennessee Representative Andy Ogles shouted, "It's your fault!" when Biden talked about fentanyl overdoses. Georgia Representative Marjorie Taylor Greene interrupted Biden many times, calling him a liar and imploring him to close the US border to prevent fentanyl deaths. The State of the Union address is considered a serious, formal occasion, and this display of disrespect for the president would have been hard to imagine in the past.

Quoted in Maegan Vazquez and Nicki Carvajal, "Republicans Repeatedly Interrupt Biden During State of the Union Address," CNN, February 8, 2023. cnn.com.

senators based their votes on merit, and especially on whether they felt the nominee could be an impartial judge. Senators often voted for candidates with different political views from their own. For example, President Ronald Reagan nominated five Supreme Court justices during the 1980s, and three of them were unanimously confirmed by the Senate.

In the current environment, this is no longer true. Senators vote with their party, regardless of the nominee's ability to be impartial. During 2017 to 2022, four Supreme Court justices were confirmed—three under the Trump administration and one under the Biden administration. In stark contrast to the unanimous votes during the Reagan years, the Senate confirmation votes were almost entirely along party lines. Republicans voted for Trump's choices and against Biden's, and Democrats did the opposite. "You see these ruthless politics where balance and rules and comity [harmony] and fairness are out the window," says Russell Robinson, a law professor at the University of California, Berkeley. "They seem to have just one concern: How do we capture the Supreme Court for our agenda? That feels wrong to a lot of people in terms of how our democracy and our Constitution should work."[12]

Extreme Polarization and Democracy

America has increasingly become a nation where people do not seek common ground with individuals outside of their silos. This is true in the everyday lives of many Americans, and it is also true in government. It poses a problem.

Democracy functions best when everyday people and politicians are willing to work together to solve community problems. "As division escalates, the normal functioning of democracy can break down if partisans cease to be able to resolve political differences by finding middle ground," argue political science professors Suzanne Mettler and Robert C. Lieberman. "Politics then instead becomes a game of moral combat in which winning is the single imperative and opponents are seen as enemies to be vanquished."[13] Extreme polarization is a warning sign that democracy is in crisis.

17

CHAPTER TWO

Misinformation and Democracy

According to social media, all kinds of remarkable things happened in early 2023. For example, contrary to what scientists have learned from their research, it turns out there is an unlimited supply of oil on the planet. Moreover, everyone can put their wallets away because cash is about to become obsolete. Not only that, but after telling everyone to wear masks during the COVID-19 pandemic, Dr. Anthony Fauci changed his mind and now says that masks do not work. (Fauci is the former director of the National Institute of Allergy and Infectious Diseases and was chief medical adviser to President Trump and President Biden.) Oh, and Budweiser is going bankrupt because of the company's support of the transgender community.

None of this is true. All of these stories have been debunked on the Associated Press website in a section titled Not Real News, which is devoted to stopping the relentless surge of misinformation on social media. And yet these stories—and many, many others of equally dubious value—have been spread widely on social media and seen by thousands of viewers.

The spread of misinformation has become extremely commonplace, especially online. "In an age where the internet is the main source of news and information for many consumers worldwide, news audiences are at higher risk than ever of encountering and sharing fake news,"[14] says Amy Watson, a senior researcher at the data analysis firm Statista. For a democracy to function well, citizens need to make informed decisions based on accurate information. The spread of misinformation is therefore a threat to democracy.

Why Information Is Important for Democracy

Because democracies are controlled by the people, democracies work best when the people are well informed. This is especially true in a representative democracy, where decisions are made by people who hold elected office. Those individuals are chosen by voters because of their background, experience, and positions on various issues. "In order for voters to make informed choices among candidates, the voters must learn about the candidates' political positions, track records, personalities, past experiences, and much more,"[15] says Stanford communication professor Jon Krosnick.

Information is also important in a democracy because it helps people keep watch over powerful people and entities in government and society. Often, the news media fulfills this role, serving as a check on the use of money, power, and influence.

> "In order for voters to make informed choices among candidates, the voters must learn about the candidates' political positions, track records, personalities, past experiences, and much more."[15]
>
> —Jon Krosnick, Stanford communication professor

Reliable information is also important in a democracy because it can reduce polarization. If people have access to accurate information about why people have different views, this promotes empathy and understanding. People tend to be less frightened of other people and ideas they understand. In contrast, lack of information or misinformation about the views of others can exacerbate the feeling of "us versus them" and can lead to violence.

Misinformation and Disinformation

Misinformation refers to any information that is false, inaccurate, or taken out of context in a way that changes its meaning. Misinformation is not always created maliciously or with the intent to

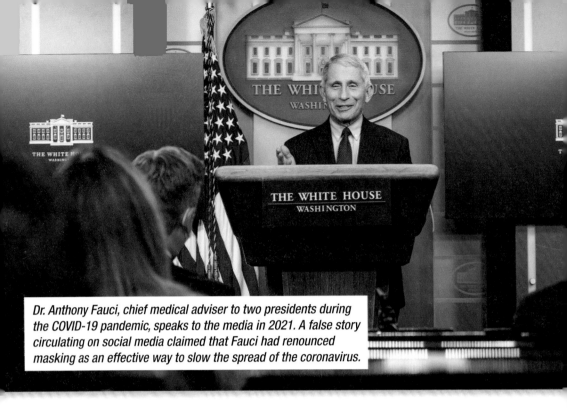

Dr. Anthony Fauci, chief medical adviser to two presidents during the COVID-19 pandemic, speaks to the media in 2021. A false story circulating on social media claimed that Fauci had renounced masking as an effective way to slow the spread of the coronavirus.

misinform. It can be a result of poor research or failure to confirm the reliability of a source. Misinformation often occurs in casual conversations when people share information that is not true—or that is true, but after the information spreads through a chain of people, the truth becomes distorted.

Disinformation is a specific kind of misinformation that is intentional and malicious. "Disinformation is content that is intentionally false and designed to cause harm," explains information expert Claire Wardle. "It is motivated by three factors: to make money; to have political influence, either foreign or domestic; or to cause trouble for the sake of it."[16]

> "Disinformation is content that is intentionally false and designed to cause harm. It is motivated by three factors: to make money; to have political influence, either foreign or domestic; or to cause trouble for the sake of it."[16]
>
> —Claire Wardle, information expert

Disinformation is often used in antidemocratic ways. In autocratic countries like North Korea, the government uses disinformation as a tool to keep itself in power, largely by controlling people's perceptions of the government. Disinformation is also used to undermine other governments through deliberate disinformation campaigns. For example, Russia has spread damaging disinformation about American political candidates who would not serve Russia's interests. Russia also spreads disinformation in order to fuel polarized political

battles, with the goal of destabilizing American democracy. "Disinformation is one of [Russia's] most important and far-reaching weapons," states the US Department of State. "Russia has operationalized the concept of perpetual adversarial competition in the information environment by encouraging the development of a disinformation and propaganda ecosystem This ecosystem creates and spreads false narratives to strategically advance the Kremlin's policy goals."[17]

Social Media and Disinformation

The explosion of the internet and social media has introduced new forms of disinformation that pose a threat to democracy. This is not to say that the internet and social media have not been *good* for democracy in other ways. The internet provides people worldwide with educational information. Social media gives people opportunities to discuss issues, learn from people with different experiences, and get involved with changing the world for the better.

However, several characteristics of the internet and social media have created an environment in which all types of misinformation—and especially disinformation—can flourish. First is the anonymity. In most cases people online can say anything without being held accountable, and people who want to spread disinformation take advantage of this. Second is the vastness of the internet and social media, where there is a seemingly endless supply of information to consume. It can be challenging to sort out fake from real. In addition, ever-evolving technology constantly gives people new ways to spread disinformation on the internet and social media by using artificial intelligence, sophisticated graphic design tools, or whatever the next innovation happens to be.

Social media platforms are designed to make it quick and easy for people to share posts, photos, and memes. This same structure also makes it easy to spread false information.

In addition, the structure of social media lends itself to the spreading of disinformation. For one thing, sharing anything on social media—memes, photos, posts full of disinformation—is easy and is built into the structure of platforms like Facebook, Twitter, and YouTube. This sharing tends to happen quickly and without much thought. People scroll, see something they like, and share without thinking critically about what they just sent. In fact, a 2023 University of California study found that people are motivated to spread disinformation for the same reasons they do anything on social media—they want to be liked and they want attention. People post and share eye-catching stories and images because they hope people will click the Like button. For influencers and others who make money based on numbers of followers and views, there is even more incentive to share this type of information.

Trolls, Bots, and Deepfakes

Three common strategies for spreading disinformation are trolls, bots, and deepfakes. Trolls are people who set up fake accounts on social media platforms. They often are employees for large companies called troll farms that are located around the world. For example, the well-known Internet Research Agency in Russia employs hundreds of professional trolls. Trolls participate in a variety of scams, including romance scams, in which trolls start fake relationships with lonely people for the purpose of extorting money. Trolls also create fake social media accounts to spread disinformation, which they try to make go viral. They work together to share each other's disinformation, and they like each other's posts continually so that social media algorithms are more likely to share these posts with real users. Trolls also congregate in chat rooms and in comments sections on many platforms, where they intentionally argue with real users about controversial issues in order to foster polarization. To appear legitimate, some trolls hijack the accounts of real users.

Bots, which are similar to trolls, are automated digital robots that are programed to mimic human behavior. They are used in industry; for example, online customer service agents are often bots. Bots are also used to spread disinformation. For example, a bot may create a fake Twitter account and post false informa-

Fox News, Dominion Voting, and Disinformation?

Social media is more commonly under attack for spreading misinformation than are traditional forms of media, like newspapers and television news. Traditional news media is more commonly criticized for *news bias* — which means that news is presented in a way that reflects a particular set of political beliefs, without presenting false information. However, in 2022 Dominion Voting Systems — a company that manufactures machines that are used to count election votes — sued Fox News for defamation. As part of Donald Trump's claims that the 2020 election was stolen, he alleged that the Dominion voting machines did not work properly and that the company intentionally deleted and altered votes. Some of the hosts on Fox News — a network that appeals to conservative viewers — presented Trump's accusations as credible facts. Dominion claimed that this was defamation, in part because Fox News hosts did not actually believe what they were saying. In 2023 emails and texts surfaced that indicated that Fox hosts like Tucker Carlson did not believe that the election was stolen, but that this was a position they needed to take publicly to appease viewers. In April 2023 the case was settled out of court, and Fox News agreed to pay Dominion $787 million dollars.

tion about a political candidate, and small armies of other bot accounts then share the tweet widely. These Twitter bots may intentionally include the candidate's campaign hashtag in their post, so that anyone looking for information on the candidate sees the disinformation. Some bots are semiautomated and are used by trolls to spread preprogrammed messages in chat rooms and comments sections.

Another common strategy is the deepfake, which is a fake image or video of a person that was created with the use of artificial intelligence and therefore looks real. Deepfakes can be used for fun; in one popular deepfake, scenes from the 2017 *Wonder Woman* movie were altered to replace lead actress Gal Gadot with images of Lynda Carter, the actress from the 1970s *Wonder Woman* TV show. However, deepfakes can be used in nefarious ways, and since people tend to believe what they see, deepfakes have the potential to be very effective. For example, in 2022, during the war between Ukraine and Russia, a deepfake was created of Ukrainian president Volodymyr Zelenskyy telling his troops to surrender. Similarly, in order to make Democratic senator Elizabeth Warren look bad, a 2022 video interview she did with Chris Hayes of MSNBC was altered so that she appears to say that Republicans should not be allowed to vote. These two videos were identified quickly as deepfakes, but as artificial intelligence evolves, deepfake technology has the potential to fool people with a dangerous glut of digital disinformation.

Conspiracy Theories and QAnon

Conspiracy theories are a form of misinformation. They are far-fetched theories about how powerful people, usually in the government, are secretly behind some sort of bizarrely nefarious scheme. Conspiracy theories are not new; for example, some people have believed for years that the 1969 moon landing never happened.

Today, thanks to the internet and social media, conspiracy theorists have the ability to spread misinformation quickly. In re-

How to Spot Deepfake Videos

How can viewers tell if a video is a deepfake? According to the MIT Media Lab, if a person appears in a video, one of the best ways to spot a deepfake is to examine the person's face carefully and look for unrealistic details. The lab's suggestions include examining the wrinkles on people's cheeks and foreheads. If the number of wrinkles does not correspond to the person's age, the video might be fake. The MIT Media Lab also suggests watching the person's blinking and lip movements, which are actions that are hard for artificial intelligence to mimic. In a deepfake, these might look unnatural. Sometimes, facial inconsistencies are easier to see by slowing down the speed of the video. Listening carefully to the video is also important. Listen for oddly mispronounced words, out-of-place background sounds, and imperfect lip-synching. Of course, one of the best tools for spotting deepfakes is critical thinking. If a video seems to portray something weird or unlikely, do some additional research to see whether the events discussed in the video are discussed on credible news sites.

cent years one of the most prolific conspiracy groups has been an extreme right-wing group called QAnon. QAnon started on social media in 2017. A user who called himself Q claimed he had secret information about Hillary Clinton and other powerful Democrats. As his following grew, Q continued to post increasingly bizarre and unsubstantiated claims.

According to QAnon, there is a secret cabal of satanic Democrats who, along with their allies, run a massive child sex-trafficking ring. In addition to raping the kidnapped children, these pedophiles supposedly harvest and drink the children's blood, which they believe will restore their youth. QAnon members believe that President Trump was secretly working behind the scenes to dismantle the cabal and that a day would come when there would be mass arrests and the cabal would be revealed to the world. Some QAnon members believe that Trump never left office and that the media is lying about Biden being the president.

QAnon lives on. In 2022 the website of the British newspaper the *Guardian* reported that about 20 percent of Americans believe that at some point soon there will be mass arrests. The *Guardian* also reported that "18% think violence might be necessary to save the country and 16% hold that the government, media and financial worlds are controlled by Satan-worshipping pedophiles."[18] QAnon sympathizers have been elected to local and national offices. Representatives Marjorie Taylor Greene of Georgia and Lauren Boebert of Colorado have, at various times, endorsed or given credence to some of the group's conspiracy theories. Other QAnon sympathizers ran for office in 2022.

According to the House of Representatives' January 6 Committee, QAnon supporters had a strong presence at the January 6 insurrection. QAnon supporters have also been involved with a number of other violent crimes. For example, in 2022 a QAnon supporter attacked the director of the National Butterfly Center in Texas because of a rumor that the center was smuggling migrants into the United States. In addition to this violence, QAnon is a threat to democracy because of its impact on the polarization of Americans. Republicans who believe that Democrats are satanic pedophiles are not going to seek common ground with them.

The Need for Accurate Information

For a democracy to flourish, citizens need reliable, accurate information. In recent years, the ability for citizens to access information has come under threat. The structure of social media and the internet has contributed to the dissemination of misinformation, disinformation, and conspiracy theories. New technology, especially artificial intelligence, has led to new opportunities for spreading disinformation, like deepfakes. When the ability to access information comes under threat, so does democracy.

CHAPTER THREE

Disrupting the Vote

Imagine a country where armed men in tactical gear gather around ballot boxes to intimidate voters, and where people who describe themselves as poll watchers stand so close to voters that they can actually read their ballot choices. Now consider this: these are not imaginary scenarios or scenes from a distant nation. Both of these incidents happened during the 2022 elections in the United States.

The ability to vote—safely, anonymously, and without fear of consequences—is one of the most fundamental requirements for a democracy. Voting is the primary mechanism that gives everyday people a voice. In recent years, democracy has been threatened by two growing trends. The first trend is the expansion of laws and regulations that restrict the ability for some people to vote or that make voting more complicated and less convenient. The second trend is an increase in intimidation and violent threats to election officials, poll workers, and voters.

Voter Restrictions or Voter Suppression?

Because democracy is, by definition, government by the people, nations become more democratic when larger numbers of people are allowed to vote—and less democratic when fewer people vote. When the United States was founded, the only people who could vote were White male landowners who were at least twenty-one years old. Today, with a few exceptions, Americans can vote if they are citizens, at least eighteen years old, and legally registered to vote in their state.

Voters cast ballots in November 2022 at a polling site in Detroit, Michigan. The ability to vote—safely, anonymously, and without fear of consequences—is one of the most fundamental requirements for a democracy.

Since 2020 many states have passed laws that make it more difficult for some people to vote. These laws affect voters in many ways. Some laws make it harder to register to vote or to vote early, while others require voters to show specific kinds of identification at polling places. The majority of these laws were passed in states with Republican-controlled legislatures.

There is substantial disagreement over the need for these laws—and for what they seek to achieve. Critics say they are harmful for democracy because they are a form of voter suppression. The League of Women Voters, a nonpartisan voter information and rights organization, defines suppression as "any attempt to prevent or discourage certain Americans from registering to vote or casting their ballot."[19] The group argues that Republicans are intentionally trying to make it harder for people in Democratic areas to vote—including people of color, who are statistically more likely to vote for Democrats. However, those who support the new laws say their goal is to preserve the democratic tradition of free and fair elections. They argue that voter fraud threatens the integrity of elections and characterize these laws as good faith attempts to prevent voter fraud.

Voter ID Laws

Voter identification laws are one of the most controversial kinds of voter restrictions. These are laws that require voters to show identification before they vote. Some states, like Minnesota, do not require voters to show identification; people can vote as long as their name is on the list of registered voters. In other states, voters do have to show identification. In less strict states, voters can use student IDs, military IDs, or similar forms of identification. However, many states are now only allowing government-issued photo ID, like a driver's license or a passport.

Critics of strict voter ID laws argue that not everyone has easy access to this kind of identification. According to the American Civil Liberties Union (ACLU), "11% of U.S. citizens—or more than 21 million Americans—do not have government-issued photo identification."[20] This includes about 25 percent of Black people of voting age, compared to only 8 percent of White people. Obtaining this kind of identification may be cost prohibitive for lower-income people.

Supporters of stronger voter ID laws say that the challenges people face in having to attain an ID are outweighed by the need to prevent voter fraud. "Voter ID laws can stop multiple types of fraud, such as impersonating another registered voter, preventing noncitizens from voting, and stopping out-of-state residents or someone registered in multiple jurisdictions,"[21] argues Fred Lucas of the Heritage Foundation, a conservative American think tank.

The ACLU argues that these laws are overly burdensome and unnecessary. It contends that voter fraud is uncommon. "In-person fraud is vanishingly rare," says the ACLU. "A recent study found that, since 2000, there were only 31 credible allegations of voter impersonation—the only type of fraud that photo IDs could prevent—during a period of time in which over 1 billion ballots were cast."[22]

> "Voter ID laws can stop multiple types of fraud, such as impersonating another registered voter, preventing noncitizens from voting, and stopping out-of-state residents or someone registered in multiple jurisdictions."[21]
>
> —Fred Lucas, Heritage Foundation

Poll workers in New York City check a voter's ID. Voter ID laws vary from state to state, with some states requiring specific forms of ID and others disallowing those same types of ID or requiring others.

Voter Purging

All states periodically update their voter lists by removing the names of people who have moved or died. However, recent laws allow states to purge large numbers of voters from their lists for other reasons. One example of this, in states like Iowa and Mississippi, are laws that call for the removal of voters who have not voted in recent elections. Supporters of these laws say that voter inactivity can be a red flag that a voter has died or moved. Critics point out that there is no law that requires people to vote in every election, and that penalizing people who choose not to vote in some elections—for any reason, including the fact that they do not like the candidates—is unfair. They also argue that these laws disproportionately impact poorer voters, who might not vote in every election because of barriers like lack of transportation.

Other states, like Arizona and Texas, have implemented strict processes to remove the names of noncitizens from voting lists. Supporters of these bills say this is important because noncitizens are not allowed to vote. Critics say these laws have resulted in the removal of many naturalized citizens, who *are* legally allowed to vote. According to Mac Brower of Democracy Docket, a publication that focuses on voter rights, tens of thousands of naturalized voters in Texas were removed in 2019 and thousands more in 2021.

Attempts to Make Voting More Difficult

Another way to suppress the vote is by making it difficult or inconvenient to vote. A common way to do this is to limit the number of polling places. This makes it harder to get to polling places and more time-intensive, because fewer polling places means longer waits at the existing ones. This disproportionally impacts socioeconomically disadvantaged voters—who are often people of color—if they do not own vehicles or cannot afford to spend hours away from work. This has a direct impact on voter turnout. "Political science research finds that voter turnout is lowest in precincts where the distance to the polling place is highest,"[23] explains political scientist Chelsea N. Jones.

Another way to make voting less convenient is to restrict early voting, which includes mail-in voting. Supporters of early voting

Voting and Disinformation

It is hard to know exactly how much disinformation there is about voting—that is, intentional efforts to prevent people from voting by disseminating false information. However, in the era of trolls, bots, and deepfakes, there is a growing concern that people will create false information to intimidate voters or to trick people into not voting—like by posting incorrect information about where polling locations are and when they are open. One notable case of disinformation occurred in 2020 when two conservative activists were accused by the Michigan Department of State and Michigan Department of the Attorney General of creating a robocall scheme to prevent people who lived in predominantly Black neighborhoods from voting by mail. The robocalls—about eighty-five thousand of them—falsely warned people that if they voted by mail, their personal information would be placed into a database that would be used by police officers, credit card companies, and government officials who wanted to force people to get vaccinated against COVID-19. In 2022 the men responsible for the robocalls were fined $5 million by the Federal Communications Commission and were ordered by a judge to spend five hundred hours registering new voters.

say that it gives people more opportunities to vote, which promotes democracy.

Critics of mail-in voting argue that it is one of the least secure methods of voting. In 2023 Arizona State Representative Alexander Kolodin—on behalf of the state Republican Party—unsuccessfully petitioned the Arizona Supreme Court to ban all mail-in voting in the state because, he stated, voters could be "coerced and intimidated to vote in a certain way when marking their ballots."[24]

This Arizona election challenge was not isolated. According to the Brennan Center for Justice, in 2023, many state legislators across the country proposed restrictions on mail-in voting. These proposed laws, the Brennan Center notes, include "new limits on who is eligible to vote by mail, set new identification requirements for requesting and returning mail ballots, [and] shorten periods for applying for or returning mail ballots."[25]

However, the Republican Party's attitude toward early voting and mail-in ballots is changing. In June 2023 the Republican National Committee announced that it would encourage rather than oppose voting by mail.

The Historical Suppression of Southern Black Voters

Between the Civil War and the passing of the Voting Rights Act in 1965, the Black vote was openly suppressed throughout the American South. Violence was one tactic. Organizations like the Ku Klux Klan used violence, including lynching, to suppress the Black vote. Laws were another tactic. Some states passed laws that said that a person could not vote unless his or her grandfather had voted. This type of law prevented most Black people from voting, because in many cases their grandfathers had been slaves and thus not allowed to vote. Southern states also prevented Black people from voting by requiring people to pay a poll tax before they could vote—an expense that many Black southerners could not afford. States also required Black voters to take literacy tests as a prerequisite for voting, which many did not pass because the tests were intentionally overcomplicated, and because many Black people in the South did not have access to a quality education. Laws like this one were repealed with the Voting Rights Act of 1965, which made it illegal to prevent people from voting because of race.

Election Workers Threatened

In addition to laws that make it harder for some people to vote, democracy is also under threat because of a dramatic increase in the use of violent threats and intimidation of election officials, poll workers, and voters. The democratic system of voting cannot exist without these three categories of people. Election officials are needed to run the election, poll workers are needed to assist voters, and voters are needed to cast ballots. Therefore, threats and intimidation meant to stop any of these activities is a threat to democracy. During the 2020 and 2022 election seasons, election officials across the country and their families were threatened and intimidated by people who believed that officials were intentionally miscounting votes or otherwise rigging the election. These threats were a widespread phenomenon. According to a March 2022 report by the Brennan Center for Justice:

> "One in six election officials have experienced threats because of their job, and 77 percent say that they feel these threats have increased in recent years."[26]
>
> —Brennan Center for Justice

One in six election officials have experienced threats because of their job, and 77 percent say that they feel these threats have increased in recent years. Ranging from death threats that name officials' young children to racist and gendered harassment, these attacks have forced election officials across the country to take steps like hiring personal security, fleeing their homes, and putting their children into counseling.[26]

Some of these threats have been very graphic, like a voice mail that was sent to an Arizona voting official in 2022 by a man who was later arrested. The voice mail said, "When we come to lynch your stupid lying Commie [expletive], you'll remember that you lied on the [expletive] Bible, you piece of [expletive]. You're gonna die, you piece of [expletive]. We're going to hang you. We're going to hang you."[27]

During the 2022 election, poll workers also dealt with intimidation. This intimidation came from people who claimed to be poll watchers but who were part of organized vigilante efforts to maintain a presence at the polls. While many poll watchers did nothing but quietly observe, others used intimidation tactics. Some poll watchers barraged workers with questions to make it difficult for them to assist voters, and others recorded poll workers without their permission. In a similar incident during New Mexico's primary election, a worker who was delivering ballots to the local clerk's office was terrified when an election watcher followed and aggressively tailgated her.

Voter Intimidation

Voters also experienced acts of intimidation during the 2022 election. Many people associate the term *voter intimidation* with violence, but violence is not the only form of voter intimidation. "Any behavior reasonably calculated to dissuade a person from participating in an election counts as intimidation," explains law professor Atiba Ellis. "This can include deceiving people about voting rules, questioning the legitimacy of their votes or accusing a person of a voting crime."[28]

According to National Public Radio, there were fewer incidents of voter intimidation in the 2022 election than authorities had feared—but there were still a number of alarming incidents. In Arizona an organized group of militia members waged a campaign outside of ballot drop boxes. Multiple uniformed, visibly armed militia members stood at ballot boxes, taking photos of voters and threatening to post images of them online with identifying information.

> "Any behavior reasonably calculated to dissuade a person from participating in an election counts as intimidation."[28]
>
> —Law professor Atiba Ellis

Other incidents included aggressive encounters between poll watchers and voters. In North Carolina poll watchers were accused of voter intimidation when they stood too close to voters. One poll watcher wedged herself be-

A California woman deposits her ballot in an official drop box. Some states have reduced the number of drop boxes available to voters. Others have eliminated them altogether.

tween a voter and a voting machine. There were also attempts to harass voters at home, like in Texas, where a local Republican Party leader knocked on the doors of people who had voted by mail and accused them of being ineligible to vote.

Another incident in Beaumont, Texas, actually involved voter intimidation by poll workers working together with the poll watchers to intimidate Black voters. According to the National Association for the Advancement of Colored People, some of the poll workers openly allowed poll watchers to stand intimidatingly close to Black people as they voted. These poll workers also refused to help Black voters insert their ballots into the machines—a service they provided to White voters.

In a democracy, people need to feel safe voting, and election officials and poll workers need to feel safe doing their jobs. Moreover, people who are legally entitled to vote need to be able to do so without laws that attempt to make this harder. Voting is one of the most fundamental rights in a democracy, and attempts to curtail this right are a serious threat to democracy.

CHAPTER FOUR

Extremist Violence

On May 14, 2022, eighty-six-year-old Ruth Whitfield was shopping at a Tops grocery store in Buffalo, New York, after visiting her husband at a nursing home. The couple had been married for sixty-eight years, and she visited him every day. "That day was like every other day for my mom,"[29] says her son Garnell Whitfield.

Ruth Whitfield was murdered in that grocery store, along with nine other people. The grocery store was in a predominantly Black neighborhood, and everyone who was killed was Black. The White shooter, eighteen-year-old Payton Gendron, shouted racial slurs as he gunned down people—half of whom were senior citizens—with a semiautomatic rifle. Gendron was motivated by extreme racism. He was a White supremacist who, in an online journal and 180-page manifesto, stated that his motive was to prevent "eliminating the white race."[30]

Perhaps the most horrifying part of this incident is that it was not all that unusual. Gendron is an example of a violent extremist—a person who uses, or threatens to use, deadly force as a tool to bring about radical changes in a society. According to the US Government Accountability Office, violent extremist incidents increased by 357 percent from 2013 to 2021. They reached a peak in 2020 and 2021 during the COVID-19 pandemic, but they are still happening at a higher rate than before 2013.

Violent extremism is prevalent for a number of reasons, including the role of the internet and social media in spreading violent ideologies, along with the availability of semiautomatic weapons. It is also prevalent because of the polarization of America. When people see political opponents as the enemy and dehumanize them, the next step for a small number of people is to take violent action.

Violent extremism in the United States is a sign of a democracy in crisis. "Political violence in the United States is a grave threat not only to the lives of Americans, but also to the health of American democracy," argues terrorism and extremism expert Daniel L. Byman. "It polarizes our already-divided country and undermines political discourse."[31]

> "Political violence in the United States is a grave threat not only to the lives of Americans, but also to the health of American democracy. It polarizes our already-divided country and undermines political discourse."[31]
>
> —Daniel L. Byman, terrorism and extremism expert

Why Violent Extremism Is a Threat to Democracy

Violent extremism is antidemocratic for a number of reasons. For one thing, it can shut down productive conversations about social issues and legislation. In a democracy, people make decisions together about governance—a process that involves debate and compromise. Violent extremism is an attempt to use violence to end the debate and to replace conversations with bullets.

Police process the scene of a 2022 mass shooting at Tops grocery story in Buffalo, New York. Authorities described the shooter as a violent extremist who was motivated by racial hatred.

Another reason violent extremism is antidemocratic is because violence makes people afraid to participate in peaceful forms of democratic action. This includes voting, attending a peaceful protest, or speaking out about political opinions. In fact, because fear is such a fundamental component of violent extremism, it is sometimes referred to as domestic terrorism.

Violent extremism is also a threat to democracy because the societal changes extremists seek are often undemocratic. For example, the people who attacked the Capitol during the January 6 insurrection were violent extremists because they used violence as a tool to overturn the results of a democratic election. Other violent extremists use violence as a tool to threaten members of minority groups—like LGBTQ people or Muslims—because they oppose the growing inclusion of these groups into the mainstream of society. Society becomes more democratic when more people are able to participate fully and speak openly about their perspectives and experiences. Extremists use violence to fight this.

White Supremacy and White Nationalism

According to the Federal Bureau of Investigation, since 2020 the majority of violent extremist acts in the United States have been motivated by racism, and primarily by White supremacy. White supremacy is the belief that White people are a genetically superior race and therefore ought to have a superior position in society. This belief overlaps with anti-Semitism, because White supremacists consider Jews to be an inferior race—along with all people of color.

Some of history's most heinous crimes have been committed in the name of White supremacy. It was used as a justification for colonialism, which began in the 1400s and continued for another five hundred years, and for the extermination of Jewish people and other minority groups during World War II. In the United States White supremacy was used to justify slavery and Native American genocide. After the Civil War it was used in the South to deny rights to Black Americans. Today many White supremacists

Bearing torches and chanting racist and anti-Semitic slurs, White supremacists and neo-Nazis march at night through the University of Virginia, Charlottesville, in 2017. The polarized US atmosphere has emboldened people with these views to speak out.

identify as White nationalists. They believe that Whites are being replaced in society by immigrants, people of color, and Jews and that Whites need to fight back to retake dominance.

White supremacy groups like the Ku Klux Klan and the American Nazi Party have mostly existed in the shadows since the civil rights era. However, in today's polarized political environment, people with these views have been emboldened to speak out. This was apparent during the Unite the Right rally in August 2017. As night fell in Charlottesville, Virginia, White supremacist groups marched with Nazi and Confederate flags and lit torches, shouting slogans like "White lives matter" and "Jews will not replace us." In an act of extremist violence, a White supremacist killed a woman as he intentionally drove his car into a crowd of people who were protesting the event.

The Unite the Right Rally and the 2022 Tops grocery store massacre were two of many instances of White supremacist violence in recent years. For example, in February 2023 two White supremacists were arrested for trying to take control of Baltimore's power grid, with the goal of inflicting damage to the majority-Black city's hospitals and businesses. Anti-Semitic attacks are up as well. In October 2018, eleven people were killed by a White nationalist as they prayed in the Tree of Life synagogue in Pittsburgh, Pennsylvania. Moreover, according to the Anti-Defamation League—an organization that fights anti-Semitism—there was a 36 percent increase in anti-Semitic harassment, vandalism, and attacks from 2021 to 2022.

Violent Extremism Based on Other Identities

Other minority groups have also been targeted by violent extremists. These include LGBTQ people, religious minorities like Muslims, immigrants, and Asian Americans. As societal norms become more accepting toward different kinds of people, extremists use violence in an attempt to change back these norms.

Violence and threats against LGBTQ people by extremist groups have increased so much that in 2022, the US Department of Homeland Security officially declared the LGBTQ community to be a domestic terrorism target. One of the worst mass shootings in American history happened in June 2016 in Orlando, Florida, at an LGBTQ nightclub called Pulse. A gunman killed forty-nine people and wounded fifty-three others. More recently, in November 2022 an LGBTQ bar was attacked in Colorado Springs, Colorado. Five people were killed and twenty-five injured, and there likely would have been many more casualties if a patron had not wrestled the gunman to the ground. Violent threats against LGBTQ Pride festivals have also increased. In June 2022 thirty-one members of the White supremacist Patriot Front group were arrested as they planned to start a riot at a Pride festival in Boise, Idaho.

In addition, violence against transgender and gender-nonconforming people is so prevalent that the Human Rights Campaign (HRC) calls it an epidemic. Every year, the HRC publishes names and photos of transgender and gender-nonconforming people who were murdered. In April 2023 there were already eleven people listed on the group's 2023 page. In addition, according to the HRC, dozens of medical professionals across the country have received violent threats because they provide treatment to help transgender patients transition.

Since the September 11, 2001, attacks, which were committed by Muslims from other countries, Muslim Americans have been the victims of extremist violence. "Muslims continue to be the target of hate, bullying, and discrimination as a result of the stereotypes that were perpetuated by Islamophobes and the media in the years following the 9/11 attacks," explains Hussam Ayloush, executive director of the Los Angeles chapter of the Council on American-Islamic Relations. "Twenty-one years after the attacks, Muslims continue to face the threat of targeted violence."[32] According to the ACLU, mosques in the United States commonly experience death threats, bomb threats, and vandalism. In December 2021 someone in a vehicle threw an explosive device into a mosque in Olympia, Washington. No one was hurt, but the blast was so loud that it could be heard 2 miles (3.2 km) away.

> "Muslims continue to be the target of hate, bullying, and discrimination as a result of the stereotypes that were perpetuated by Islamophobes and the media in the years following the 9/11 attacks."[32]
>
> —Hussam Ayloush, Council on American-Islamic Relations

Violence Against Politicians

Violent threats and actual violence against politicians have increased dramatically since 2016. In 2021, according to the US Capitol Police, there were over nine thousand recorded threats on members of Congress. Both Republicans and Democrats have been attacked. In 2017 a left-wing extremist targeted Republican members of Congress who were practicing for the annual bipartisan congressional baseball game the next day. Six people were shot, including US House majority whip Steve Scalise, who was critically injured. In June 2022 an armed man with the intent to kill Supreme Court justice Brett Kavanaugh was arrested outside of the justice's house. In October 2022 an intruder broke into the home of Speaker of the House Nancy Pelosi, with the intent of holding Pelosi hostage, interrogating her, and breaking her kneecaps. Pelosi was not home, and the intruder severely injured her eighty-two-year-old husband with a hammer.

Violent extremists often are anti-immigrant and are especially hostile to immigrants from Latin American countries. In August 2019, after posting an anti-immigrant manifesto online, a gunman killed twenty-three people and injured twenty-three others at a Walmart in El Paso, Texas, a border town with a large immigrant population. In early 2023, in anticipation of an expected surge of immigrants at the US-Mexico border, the US Department of Homeland Security tracked hundreds of violent online conversations that discussed tactics for stopping immigrants, including luring them into trailers filled with gas.

Extremist Violence from Militia Groups

Extremist violence is also on the rise from members of militia groups. Militias are private, heavily armed paramilitary organizations. Members train each other to use weapons and military tactics. Militia members see themselves as an army of citizens who work together to protect the public. "People in militias believe it is their constitutional duty as good Americans to be heavily armed and prepared to defend themselves, their families and their country against threats ranging from natural disasters to foreign invasion," says Amy Cooter, a sociologist who studies militias. "They join to practice and share skills related to target shooting, land navigation and general emergency preparedness."[33] Most, but not all, militia members are conservative and strongly distrust the government.

Militia groups are not all the same, and many militia members are not violent. However, as Cooter explains, in recent years, many militias have become more extreme in their antigovernment beliefs. "I have observed an increase in extremism in recent years, with people who used to focus on camaraderie and preparedness at militia events now echoing claims that the insurrection at the Capitol was nothing more than a protest," says Cooter. "Others repeatedly posted on social media about the need to personally 'do something' about the supposedly stolen presidential election."[34]

During the COVID-19 pandemic, many militia members were enraged about lockdowns and mandatory mask mandates, which they viewed as tyrannical government overreach. In an extreme example of this, in October 2020 members of the Wolverine Watchmen were arrested for plotting to kidnap Michigan governor Gretchen Whitmer because of her COVID-19 policies.

> "I have observed an increase in extremism in recent years, with people who used to focus on camaraderie and preparedness at militia events now echoing claims that the insurrection at the Capitol was nothing more than a protest."[34]
>
> —Amy Cooter, a sociologist who studies militias

Angry about lockdowns and mask mandates during the pandemic, one extremist group plotted to kidnap Michigan governor Gretchen Whitmer (pictured). The leaders of this plot were given multiyear prison sentences.

This was part of a larger plan to overthrow the Michigan state government. The coleaders of this plot were sentenced to sixteen and nineteen years in prison, respectively.

According to the House of Representatives' January 6 Committee, militia groups were responsible for planning much of the January 6 insurrection. In the months leading up to January 6, groups like the Oath Keepers and the Proud Boys coordinated efforts online to try to prevent the certification of the election. As January 6 approached, they rallied members and recruited like-minded people to come to Washington, DC, bring weapons, and prepare for violence. They shared blueprints of the US Capitol Building. "We aren't getting through this without a civil war," wrote Stewart Rhodes, the leader of the Oath Keepers, in a text to fellow militia members. "Too late for that. Prepare your mind, body, spirit."[35] On January 6 the Proud Boys group was the first to dismantle the barricades at the Capitol and break in.

Although many militia leaders were arrested and imprisoned for their role in the January 6 insurrection, Cooter warns that militias still pose a dangerous threat to democracy. Since the insurrection, militia groups have become harder to track because they have gotten better at hiding their online communications. "I don't think that Jan. 6 is the end of the story," says Cooter. "I'm quite concerned about the activities that we'll see headed into the next presidential election cycle in particular."[36]

Violence and the Future of Democracy

People who replace democratic debate with violence and who fight for social change not with words but with bullets and threats are a danger to democracy. They exacerbate the already dangerous levels of political polarization and scare people away from participating in democracy in nonviolent ways. Extremist violence is not compatible with democracy.

CHAPTER FIVE

How Young Americans Can Help Save Democracy

On March 23, 2023, there was a mass shooting at an American school. In Nashville, Tennessee, a gunman walked into a parochial elementary school and murdered three nine-year-old children and three adults. The shooting was horrifying—and so was the fact that it was not a surprise. According to the *Washington Post*, from April 1999 to May 2023, there were 360 school shootings in the United States. In 2022 alone, there were 46 school shootings. Students across America have grown up with active-shooter drills.

A week after the Nashville shooting, thousands of students in the area walked out of class and gathered at the state capitol building to demand stronger gun laws. "I want to be part of this and make change in our society, because we sure need it,"[37] said Clara Thorsen, a high school student at the protest. Students in thousands of schools across the country walked out as well. The protest was organized by March for Our Lives, an organization started in 2018 by survivors of a high school shooting in Parkland, Florida.

Can young people make a difference in the fight for democracy? As daunting as today's issues may be, young Americans share a number of characteristics that may empower them to help make the United States a more democratic nation.

March for Our Lives was created by the teenage survivors of the deadly 2018 mass shooting in Parkland, Florida. Since then, the group has organized protests and sought changes in gun laws. Pictured here is a 2018 protest in Columbia, South Carolina.

Why Young People Can Help Save Democracy

Today's young people—Generation Z (born 1996 to 2012) and Generation Alpha (born 2012 to 2025)—are different from past generations in several important ways. Unlike their parents and grandparents, they are digital natives. They cannot remember a time before transformative technologies like smartphones, computers, streaming services, and social media, and they are adept at using these technologies. Young Americans are also more diverse than older Americans. According to the Pew Research Center, almost half of all Gen Zers are people of color—a sharp increase from previous generations—and about 20 percent of them identify as LGBTQ.

One reason why today's youth are in a position to fight for change is that no one has to convince them that changes are needed. While older Americans also faced enormous challenges—like racial segregation and war—youth and politics expert John

Della Volpe argues that young Americans have dealt with an exceptional amount of trauma at a young age. "This is a generation that's dealt with more trauma more quickly than any generation in 70 years," explains Della Volpe. "All that trauma happened before the oldest member of this generation turned 25, when neuroscience tells us that our brains are mature."[38] Young people's lives were severely disrupted by the COVID-19 pandemic, which had a huge impact on their education and mental health. Their childhood memories include school shootings, the videotaped murder of George Floyd, the January 6 insurrection, and dire warnings about the health of the planet. They do not know what it is like to grow up in an America without extreme political polarization.

Young people are also positioned to make change because they have the most at stake. Some of the issues that polarize Americans the most—student loan debt, health care reform, abortion, opioid abuse—are ones that directly impact today's youth. In addition, as they get older, young people are likely to struggle with the crippling costs of housing, health care, college education, and child care.

Perhaps because of this, young people in general are more politically aware and less apathetic than young people in the past. In the 2020 and 2022 elections, record numbers of people under age twenty-five voted. "I used to think politics was a bunch of

Filming George Floyd

An example of a young person who made an international impact is Darnella Frazier. On May 25, 2020, the seventeen-year-old filmed on her cell phone the murder of George Floyd under the knee of a police officer in Minneapolis. Frazier had walked to the convenience store with her younger cousin for snacks. A crowd was gathering on the sidewalk as Officer Derek Chauvin pinned Floyd on the street by lodging his knee on Floyd's neck. Frazier filmed the incident and then posted the video on Facebook and Instagram. The video went viral and started a worldwide movement to protest police violence against Black people. If Frazier had not filmed the murder, the officer's original police report—which said that Floyd had died due to medical distress—would have stood. Frazier later testified at Chauvin's trial, where he was sentenced to prison for twenty-two and a half years.

noise that didn't matter," says Iris Zhan, a Gen Z activist. "But like members of my generation, we grew up from a young age in a world that forced us to be political. I grew up watching the news instead of watching American TV classics."[39]

Della Volpe agrees that many young people today are politically aware and active. He says:

> We are seeing young Americans increasingly motivated to engage in politics out of sheer self-defense and a responsibility to fight for those even more vulnerable than themselves. Every major political battle in America has Gen Z in the middle of it. This generation has a fire and urgency unlike any I've seen in 20 years, and they expect their elected officials and candidates to show the same.[40]

In addition, young people may have the ability to break down political polarization, because as a diverse generation, they tend to be more empathetic and accepting of others than previous

In 2020 in Miami, Florida, many people—including many young adults—cast ballots or await their turn to vote. Record numbers of people under twenty-five voted in the 2020 and 2022 elections.

generations have been. "I think that maybe Gen Z is just kinder," explains Isabella D'Alacio, a recent college graduate. "I think that's something that we all really collectively value, and it's not something to be mistaken for weakness or sensitivity. It's acceptance, and it's love, and I think Gen Z has a lot of radical love."[41]

Young people cannot be expected to end the threats to democracy alone. However, there are ways for young people to get involved that can make a difference.

> "We are seeing young Americans increasingly motivated to engage in politics out of sheer self-defense and a responsibility to fight for those even more vulnerable than themselves."[40]
>
> —John Della Volpe, youth and politics expert

Being an Educated and Informed Consumer

Because decisions in a democracy are made by the people, it works best when people are well educated about government, history, civics, and current events. "History matters, as does an understanding of our government and how it works," argues journalist Nicholas Goldberg. "Especially in times like these. We're an increasingly polarized country in an increasingly globalized world—and only with informed and engaged citizens can a democracy like ours function."[42]

Unfortunately, many Americans are not well educated on these issues. According to the National Assessment of Educational Progress, only 13 percent of eighth graders in 2023 were proficient in US history, and only 22 percent were proficient in civics. Moreover, according to a 2022 University of Pennsylvania survey, older Americans also lack knowledge about these issues. For example, less than half of all US adults can name all three branches of government.

One of the most helpful things young people can do to preserve democracy is to be informed. Courses in contemporary US and world history are a great place to start, along with government, economics, women's studies, ethnic studies, and critical media studies. Reading about history, politics, and current events is also helpful—and not just in books. While disinformation on

49

the internet damages democracy, the internet is also an asset to democracy because it is also full of good information. Well-respected newspapers from around the world—and from local communities—can be found online, along with online news sites that have earned a reputation for accurate and in-depth reporting.

People can also stay informed by seeking out information in their communities, like by attending school board or city council meetings. Local politicians sometimes conduct listening sessions at which they discuss local issues.

Be a Media-Literate Consumer

Media literacy is the ability to critically analyze the contents of news, popular culture, advertisements, and other media. Critically analyzing news and other information is an important part of being well informed.

There are a few questions readers can ask when analyzing news. First, is this source accurate? A good way to confirm this is to compare the source to other news sources. Checking websites like FactCheck.org and Snopes can also verify the accuracy of a source.

Second, is this source biased? News is never a simple snapshot of the world. Decisions always have to be made at a news organization about how to present an issue. Many news organizations tend to present news stories through a particular worldview—conservative, liberal, pro-business, religious, feminist, or something else. Readers can get a sense of a media outlet's biases by browsing headlines and other articles. One of the best ways to navigate news bias is to read multiple sources about the same issue and examine how the information in each source is presented differently.

Third, it is important to be able to identify disinformation. Be aware of the presence of trolls, bots, and deepfakes—and keep informed about new forms of disinformation, since these tactics are always evolving. Be careful to not contribute to disinformation by sharing it on social media without verifying the accuracy of the information.

Vote—and Support Voting

Voting in local, state, and federal elections is one of the best ways to promote democracy. Although voting rates among young people climbed during the 2020 and 2022 elections, voting rates are still way higher for older people. Politicians tend to focus on issues that their voters care about, so they focus more on issues that affect older Americans (like Social Security) and less on issues that affect younger ones (like youth mental health issues). This will change if more young people vote.

Working to increase voter turnout is also a way that young people can help support democracy, even if they cannot yet vote themselves. Political parties and campaigns spend time trying to get more people to vote, and anyone can contact these groups and volunteer to help. This could mean sending postcards to registered voters reminding them to vote or handing out flyers at an event with information on how to register.

Young people can also encourage people in their lives to vote—including other young people. In St. Louis Park, Minnesota, seniors Isaac Israel and Sebastian Tangelson started a voter registration drive at their high school in 2022. In addition to sharing information online and in person about how to register, they

Fighting for Teenage Vote

Will sixteen-year-old Americans one day be allowed to vote? In 2020 high school students in Oakland, California, campaigned to give sixteen- and seventeen-year-olds the right to vote in school board elections. "It's always the adults making decisions on behalf of us," said seventeen-year-old Rochelle Berdan, who was part of the Oakland Youth Vote organization that led the campaign. "We deserve to have a say in the things that impact us." The students were able to get the issue on the local ballot, and 67 percent of Oakland voters agreed that young people should be allowed to vote in the 2022 school board election. However, Alameda County refused to implement the measure, saying it needed more time to make the change. Oakland Youth Vote continues to fight for the rights of students to vote in school board elections.

Quoted in Moriah Balingit, "These Teens Won the Right to Vote. Their County Disenfranchised Them," *Washington Post*, November 30, 2022. www.washingtonpost.com.

kicked off the registration drive with a school assembly. Speakers included Minnesota state representative Larry Kraft and lieutenant governor Peggy Flanagan. The two officials spoke to students about the importance of voting and civic engagement—both of which were the focus of Israel and Tangelson's efforts. "Actions like this (kickoff) to get kids registered are a smart way to get people involved,"[43] explains Israel.

Be an Involved Citizen

In addition to voting, there are actions that people can take to promote democracy. One way is by supporting political candidates who support democracy. Contact campaigns to see what kind of volunteer help they need. Campaigns also need donations, and even small ones matter because they add up. When looking for candidates to support, consider local ones.

Another way that everyday people can get involved is to attend a peaceful protest or march. At a protest, volunteers may be asked to make or carry signs, chant slogans (like "This is what democracy looks like!"), and sign up to volunteer with the organization holding the protest. People have the right to peacefully protest, and most protests are safe and free of violence. However, keep in mind that there is sometimes a risk of encounters with angry counterprotesters. Websites like that of the ACLU have information about what to expect at protests and how to stay safe.

High school and middle school students sometimes organize their own protests. In February 2023 high school students in Collingswood, New Jersey, walked out of school and protested what they felt was the discriminatory treatment of Black students. Students walked out for three days, with over one hundred students participating the first day. "I believe that it was only right if I stood up for what I believe in, stand up for my fellow students, myself," says sophomore Isabela Brown. "I think the walkout was very important to show the school and

High school and middle school students sometimes organize protests on campus for issues that deeply concern them. In 2022 students in Saint Paul, Minnesota, held a walkout to demand justice for Amir Locke, who was fatally shot by a Minneapolis police officer.

the staff how we actually feel and how much we actually care about this situation."[44] In response, the district administration held a three-hour town hall meeting and pledged to investigate the students' concerns and invest in inclusivity measures at the school.

Protecting Democracy Every Day

Young people can also help fight for democracy in their everyday lives. They can speak out when they hear someone make ugly comments about a person's race, gender identity, or religion. This includes jokes. This is not always easy, but if enough people speak out, things may change.

Another important thing that everyday people can do for democracy is listen to voices outside of their political silos—by reading things written from a different perspective or speaking to people online or in person. Listen with an empathetic ear, and try to understand why people with this perspective feel the way they do.

Do Not Give Up

America is going through a frightening time. It can be easy for people to feel like nothing can be done. However, if things are going to change, people have to believe they *can* change. "Democracy depends on hope and possibility," writes Protect Democracy, a nonprofit organization that fights authoritarian attacks on democracy. "The most important tools we have are our optimism, willingness to trust and collaborate, openness to possibility, and strength in diversity. Democracy is, at its core, nothing less and nothing more than the conviction that, together, we can build a better world than any one of us could design on our own."[45]

> "Democracy depends on hope and possibility. The most important tools we have are our optimism, willingness to trust and collaborate, openness to possibility, and strength in diversity."[45]
>
> —Protect Democracy, a nonprofit organization that fights authoritarian attacks on democracy

Introduction: A Crisis Point for American Democracy

1. Quoted in Mariel Padilla, "'I'm Running for My Life. I Cannot Talk to You Right Now': 23 Women in Congress Recall the Capitol Riot," The 19th, February 12, 2021. www.19thnews.org.
2. Quoted in Tom Jackman, "Capitol Police Officer Caroline Edwards Recounts Jan. 6 'War Scene,'" *Washington Post*, June 10, 2022. www.washingtonpost.com.
3. Quoted in Alvin Powell, "Where Are We Going, America?," *Harvard Gazette*, November 4, 2022. https://news.harvard.edu.

Chapter One: A Polarized Nation

4. Quoted in Brittany Wong, "The Advice Therapists Give People Considering Severing Ties with Their Family Over Politics," Huffington Post, January 20, 2023. www.huffpost.com.
5. Pew Research Center, "As Partisan Hostility Grows, Signs of Frustration with the Two Party System," August 9, 2022. www.pewresearch.org.
6. Chicago1Ray (@Chicago1Ray), "Fact is, there's way more evidence that points to the fact that Trump won," Twitter, May 8, 2023, 9:45 a.m. https://twitter.com/Chicago1Ray/status/1655584771857104899.
7. Vince (@borosup90), "Facts are the facts," Twitter, May 7, 2023, 10:45 p.m. https://twitter.com/borosup90/status/1653606668310020096.
8. Richard Groves, "Richard Groves: Let's Stop Hiding Behind the Hardened Walls of Our Silos," *Winston-Salem (NC) Journal*, April 30, 2023. www.journalnow.com.
9. Quoted in Deepa Shivaram and Emily Olson, "Sanders Says the Choice in the U.S. Is 'Normal or Crazy' in GOP Response to Biden," National Public Radio, February 8, 2023. www.npr.org.
10. Quoted in Thomas B. Edsall, "How to Tell When Your Country Is Past the Point of No Return," *New York Times*, December 15, 2021. www.nytimes.com.
11. Quoted in Allan Smith, "McConnell Says He's '100 Percent' Focused on 'Stopping' Biden's Administration," NBC News, May 5, 2021. www.nbcnews.com.
12. Quoted in Edward Lempinen, "Voting, Race, and Religion: Is the U.S. Supreme Court a Threat to Democracy?," Berkeley News, March 9, 2023. https://news.berkeley.edu.
13. Suzanne Mettler and Robert C. Lieberman, *Four Threats: Recurring Crises of American Democracy*. New York: St. Martin's, 2020, p. 17.

Chapter Two: Misinformation and Democracy

14. Amy Watson, "Fake News Worldwide—Statistics & Facts," Statista, July 8, 2022. www.statista.com.
15. Quoted in Sandra Feder, "Stanford Researchers Discuss Journalism and Democracy in Lead-Up to Super Tuesday," Stanford News, February 27, 2020. https://news.stanford.edu.
16. Claire Wardle, "Understanding Information Disorder," First Draft News, September 22, 2020. https://firstdraftnews.org.
17. US Department of State, "Disarming Disinformation: Our Shared Responsibility," May 1, 2023. www.state.gov.
18. David Smith, "Belief in QAnon Has Strengthened in U.S. Since Trump Was Voted Out, Study Finds," *The Guardian* (Manchester, UK), February 24, 2022. www.theguardian.com.

Chapter Three: Disrupting the Vote

19. League of Women Voters. "Fighting Voter Suppression: Why It Matters," 2022. www.lwv.org.
20. American Civil Liberties Union, "Oppose Voter ID Legislation—Fact Sheet," 2023. www.aclu.org.
21. Fred Lucas, "Voter ID Laws Are Popular for Good Reason," Heritage Foundation, January 17, 2023. www.heritage.org.
22. American Civil Liberties Union, "Oppose Voter ID Legislation—Fact Sheet."
23. Chelsea N. Jones, "States Are Closing Polling Places. That Hurts Democracy," *Washington Post*, June 17, 2022. www.washingtonpost.com.
24. Quoted in Bob Christie, "Scottsdale Lawyer Loses GOP Legal Bid to End Early Voting in Arizona," *Phoenix Daily Independent*, June 3, 2023. www.yourvalley.net.
25. Brennan Center for Justice, "Voting Laws Roundup: February 2023," February 27, 2023. www.brennancenter.org.
26. Ruby Edlin and Turquoise Baker, "Poll of Local Election Officials Finds Safety Fears for Colleagues—and Themselves," Brennan Center for Justice, March 10, 2022. www.brennancenter.org.
27. Quoted in Perry Vandell, "Iowa Man Pleads Guilty to Sending Death Threats to Arizona Election Official," *Arizona Republic* (Phoenix), April 13, 2023. www.azcentral.com.
28. Atiba Ellis, "Voter Intimidation in 2022 Follows a Long History of Illegal, and Racist, Bullying," The Conversation, November 14, 2022. www.theconversation.com.

Chapter Four: Extremist Violence

29. Quoted in Carolyn Thompson, "For Buffalo Shooting Victims and Survivors, It Was 'like Every Other Day,'" *PBS NewsHour*. May 17, 2022. www.pbs.org.

30. Quoted in Associated Press, "Buffalo Shooting Suspect Says His Motive Was to Prevent 'Eliminating the White Race,'" National Public Radio, June 16, 2022. www.npr.org.

31. Daniel L. Byman, "Countering Organized Violence in the United States," Brookings Institution, May 16, 2023. www.brookings.edu.

32. Hussam Ayloush, "Decades After 9/11, Muslims Battle Islamophobia in US," Al Jazeera, September 11, 2022. www.aljazeera.com.

33. Amy Cooter, "Citizen Militias in the U.S. Are Moving Towards More Violent Extremism," *Scientific American*, January 1, 2022. www.scientificamerican .com.

34. Cooter, "Citizen Militias in the U.S. Are Moving Towards More Violent Extremism."

35. Quoted in Sarah N. Lynch and Chris Gallagher, "Factbox: Key Quotes Cited as Evidence of Seditious Conspiracy in U.S. Trial of Oath Keepers," Reuters, October 11, 2022. www.abcnews.com.

36. Quoted in Alysha Webb et al., "How Has Domestic Terrorism Changed 2 Years After Jan. 6," ABC News, January 6, 2023. www.abcnews.go.com.

Chapter Five: How Young Americans Can Help Save Democracy

37. Quoted in Marta W. Aldrich, "Nashville Students Rally for Tougher Gun Laws, as Governor Seeks Armed Guards for Every School," Chalkbeat Tennessee, April 3, 2023. tn.chalkbeat.org.

38. Quoted in Christina Pazzanese, "Rising Political Tide of Young Adults, Gen Z," *Harvard Gazette*, April 14, 2023. https://news.harvard.edu.

39. Iris Zhan, "'Shaping This World'—How Gen Z Is Getting More Engaged in Politics than Ever," Common Cause, May 3, 2023. www.commoncause .org.

40. Quoted in Harvard Kennedy School Institute of Politics, "Harvard Youth Poll," Spring 2023. iop.harvard.edu.

41. Quoted in *New York Times*, "'Maybe Gen Z Is Just Kinder': How America's Youngest Voters Are Shaping Politics," October 26, 2022. www.nytimes .com.

42. Nicholas Goldberg, "When Students Don't Understand History, What Are Democracy's Chances?," *Los Angeles Times*, May 15, 2023. www.la times.org.

43. Quoted in Maya Nieves, "High Hopes for Youth Participation in Upcoming Election," Echo, October 1, 2022. https://slpecho.com.

44. Quoted in Brianna Kudisch, "Student Protests at N.J. High School Lead to Discussions About Racism, Sexual Assault Allegations," NJ.com, February 23, 2023. www.nj.com.

45. Protect Democracy, "How to Protect Democracy," 2023. https://protect democracy.org.

News Literacy Project

http://newslit.org

The News Literacy Project is a nonpartisan educational organization that offers resources to teachers, students, and others on how to become a more literate news consumer. Its site features "Get Smart About News" posts that contain recent information about issues like disinformation and news bias.

Not Real News, Associated Press

https://apnews.com/hub/not-real-news

A project of the Associated Press, Not Real News debunks fake news stories and graphics that have been shared widely on social media, with clear explanations of why each news story is false. The site is a good resource in the fight against misinformation.

Rock the Vote

https://rockthevote.org

Rock the Vote is an organization that encourages young people to vote and become more politically active. Its website contains information about ways that young people can volunteer to help with voter turnout efforts.

Southern Poverty Law Center

www.splcenter.org

The Southern Poverty Law Center is an organization that fights White supremacy. The center monitors extremist groups in the United States and exposes their activity to law enforcement and the public.

Voting Rights Project, American Civil Liberties Union

www.aclu.org/issues/voting-rights

The American Civil Liberties Union provides information about the civil rights of Americans and fights legal battles on behalf of people whose rights have been violated. Much of its work is devoted to defending voting rights. Its Voting Rights Project website provides information about recent voting rights legislation.

Books

Kate Alexander, *Generation Brave: The Gen Z Kids Who Are Changing the World*. Kansas City, MO: Andrews McMeel, 2020.

Donald A. Barclay, *Disinformation: The Nature of Facts and Lies in the Post-truth Era*. Lanham, MD: Rowman & Littlefield, 2022.

Arthur Blaustein, *Democracy Is Not a Spectator Sport: The Ultimate Civic Engagement Handbook*. New York: Skyhorse, 2020.

Daryl Johnson, *Hateland: A Long, Hard Look at America's Extremist Heart*. Amherst, NY: Prometheus, 2021.

Suzanne Mettler and Robert C. Lieberman, *Four Threats: The Recurring Crises on American Democracy*. New York: St. Martin's, 2020.

Elizabeth Rusch, *You Call This Democracy? How to Fix Our Government and Deliver Power to the People*. Boston: Houghton Mifflin Harcourt, 2020.

John Della Volpe, *FIGHT: How Gen Z Is Channeling Their Fear & Passion to Save America*. New York: St. Martin's, 2022.

Kevin Winn, *Voting Rights*. Ann Arbor, MI: Cherry Lake, 2022.

Internet Sources

Adrienne LaFrance, "The New Anarchy: America Faces a Type of Extremist Violence It Does Not Know How to Stop," *The Atlantic*, March 6, 2023. www.theatlantic.com.

David Leonhardt, "'A Crisis Coming: The Twin Threats to American Democracy,'" *New York Times*, September 21, 2022. www.nytimes.com.

Shawna Mizells, "Lawmakers in 32 States Have Introduced Bills to Restrict Voting So Far This Legislative Session," CNN, February 22, 2023. www.cnn.com.

New York Times Editorial Board, "America Can Have Democracy or Political Violence. Not Both," *New York Times*, November 3, 2022. www.nytimes.com.

Miles Parks and Shannon Bond, "AI Deepfakes Could Advance Misinformation in the Run Up to the 2024 Election," National Public Radio, March 26, 2023. www.npr.org.

Brittany Wong, "The Advice Therapists Give People Considering Severing Ties with Family over Politics," Huffington Post, January 20, 2023. www.huffpost.com.

ABOUT THE AUTHOR

Naomi Rockler is an educational freelance writer who writes non-fiction and fiction books for teenagers. She lives in Minnesota with her husband and daughter.